John Whittaker Watson

Beautiful Snow

And other Poems

John Whittaker Watson

Beautiful Snow
And other Poems

ISBN/EAN: 9783337258054

Printed in Europe, USA, Canada, Australia, Japan

Cover: Foto ©Thomas Meinert / pixelio.de

More available books at **www.hansebooks.com**

AND

OTHER POEMS.

BY

J. W. WATSON.

NEW AND ENLARGED EDITION.

PHILADELPHIA:
T. B. PETERSON & BROTHERS;
306 CHESTNUT STREET.

TO MY MOTHER.

CONTENTS.

	PAGE
BEAUTIFUL SNOW	7
THE SUNLIGHT IN HER HAIR	12
NO LETTER	16
A MILLION, ALL IN GOLD	20
DEATH'S CARRIAGE STOPS THE WAY	25
MY PIPE	30
THE DYING SOLDIER	36
THE SAILING OF THE YACHTS	42
"RING DOWN THE DROP—I CANNOT PLAY."	46
THE OLDEST PAUPER ON THE TOWN	50
DROWNED	55
THE SKATERS	61
GIVE ME DRINK	68
"IT WILL ALL BE RIGHT IN THE MORNING."	72
GOD BLESS YOUR BEAUTIFUL HAND	75
FARMER BROWN	78
THE PATTER OF LITTLE FEET	83

CONTENTS.

OLD NEWS	87
MISSING: PRIVATE WILLIAM SMITH	94
I WISH THAT I COULD RUN AWAY	97
THE KISS IN THE STREET	101
"I WOULD THAT SHE WERE DEAD!"	104
WHAT I SAW	111
"PLEASE HELP THE BLIND"	116
SOMEWHERE TO GO	120
SWINGING IN THE DANCE	125

BEAUTIFUL SNOW.

OH! the snow, the beautiful snow,
    Filling the sky and the earth below:
Over the house-tops, over the street,
Over the heads of the people you meet;
      Dancing,
          Flirting,
              Skimming along.
Beautiful snow! it can do nothing wrong.
Flying to kiss a fair lady's cheek;
Clinging to lips in a frolicsome freak.
Beautiful snow, from the heavens above,
Pure as an angel and fickle as love!

Oh! the snow, the beautiful snow!
How the flakes gather and laugh as they go!

Whirling about in its maddening fun,
It plays in its glee with every one.
   Chasing,
     Laughing,
       Hurrying by,
It lights up the face and it sparkles the eye;
And even the dogs, with a bark and a bound,
Snap at the crystals that eddy around.
The town is alive, and its heart in a glow
To welcome the coming of beautiful snow.

How the wild crowd goes swaying along,
Hailing each other with humor and song!
How the gay sledges like meteors flash by—
Bright for a moment, then lost to the eye.
   Ringing,
     Swinging,
       Dashing they go
Over the crest of the beautiful snow:

Snow so pure when it falls from the sky,
To be trampled in mud by the crowd rushing by;
To be trampled and tracked by the thousands of feet
Till it blends with the horrible filth in the street.

Once I was pure as the snow—but I fell:
Fell, like the snow-flakes, from heaven — to hell:
Fell, to be tramped as the filth of the street:
Fell, to be scoffed, to be spit on and beat.
  Pleading,
    Cursing,
      Dreading to die,
Selling my soul to whoever would buy,
Dealing in shame for a morsel of bread,
Hating the living and fearing the dead.
Merciful God! have I fallen so low?
And yet I was once like this beautiful snow!

Once I was fair as the beautiful snow,
With an eye like its crystals, a heart like its glow;
Once I was loved for my innocent grace—
Flattered and sought for the charm of my face.
    Father,
        Mother,
            Sisters all,
God, and myself, I have lost by my fall.
The veriest wretch that goes shivering by
Will take a wide sweep, lest I wander too nigh;
For of all that is on or about me, I know
There is nothing that's pure but the beautiful snow.

How strange it should be that this beautiful snow
Should fall on a sinner with nowhere to go!
How strange it would be, when the night comes again,
If the snow and the ice struck my desperate brain!

   Fainting,

    Freezing,

     Dying alone

Too wicked for prayer, too weak for my moan

To be heard in the crash of the crazy town,

Gone mad in its joy at the snow's coming down;

To lie and to die in my terrible woe,

With a bed and a shroud of the beautiful snow!

THE SUNLIGHT IN HER HAIR.

THERE'S an old stone house, on a lonely street—
  A house of a sombre hue—
And day by day, for forty years,
  I've passed within its view;
A house of a dead and mouldy state—
The cast-off shell of the rich and great—
  It frowns on the street, through its dingy paint,
    In a consequential way;
  Seeming to shrink from the summer air
    And the yellow sunlight's play.

But I watch alone the one bright spot
  On those dingy, sombre walls,
Where a woman sits at her daily toil,
  And the yellow sunlight falls.

I have watched that window for forty years,
Through the breaking of smiles and the falling
of tears;
I have watched the jewel my heart has en
shrined,
And my daily prayers bless;
I have mingled her name with my nightly
dreams—
Fair Josephine Van Ness.

And never, in all these long, long years,
Have I spoken to Josephine,
But I watch the sunlight play in her hair
And the shadows pass between;
And I muse on the change that time will bring
To every fair and beautiful thing;
For when first the sunlight fell on her hair
It played with each golden braid;
But the gold has gone, and the gathered locks
Are with lines of silver laid.

I never have spoken to Josephine,
  Though I've loved her long and well;
But the dreams I have dreamed of the coming time
  Are more than my heart can tell.
I have promised myself from day to day,
Till my step has grown old and my hair has grown gray,
  That when fortune shall favor my efforts to rise,
  Dear Josephine shall share,
And the dim old house shall be bright again
  With the sunlight in her hair.

She may have grown old to other eyes—
  To mine she is ever the same,
Like a glorious picture mellowed by time,
  And set in an oaken frame.
For many and many a toilsome year
I lingered in passion, or shivered in fear,

Lest some who were greater or richer than I
   Should mark the yellow sheen
Of the sunlight dancing in her hair,
   And woo my Josephine.

But the years have passed us, one by one,
   And never a wooer there came;
They may have slighted the toiling girl,
   But I love her just the same.
And every day I will pass the street,
Though she hears not the sound of my lingering
      feet;
And every day, through the winter's snow,
   And summer's waving green,
I will look at the window, and wait for the time
   I can speak to Josephine.

NO LETTER.

OH HOPE! thou stolid tenant of
   Each wayworn wanderer's worldly breast,
Can no alarms before thy gate
   Erect once more thy warrior crest?
Hath love and fortune, long deferred,
   So palsied all thy limbs of steel
That life hath nothing in its creed
   To rouse thee up for woe or weal?

With listless feet and vacant air,
   On distant shores I mark my round,
And scan with careless eye the crowds
   I meet on unfamiliar ground.
Not gaining by my worldly lore,
   Not profiting by stranger hands,

NO LETTER.

My heart goes back through weary miles
  To clasp the love of other lands.

One daily pilgrimage I tread,
  The Mecca of my stolid hope,
One path in utter darkness veiled,
  With hands outstretched, I daily grope.
Before a portal, prison barred,
  My shibboleth I daily sum,
And watch a youth hold countless worlds
  Between a finger and a thumb.

I watch with eager eyes his face,
  On which unmeaning silence broods,
Bent o'er the eloquence of man
  In all his wondrous human moods.
I chafe when, like some mere machine,
  On Beauty's missive falls his touch,
And wonder why electric force
  Should not unloose the vampyre clutch.

Life, love and death, beneath his hand,
  Run glib and facile to and fro;
Stark, staring ruin, sudden wealth,
  Like flashing meteors come and go.
The fierce defiance, greed of gold,
  The cry for mercy—softly cried—
And one faint, wandering line from him
  Who on the field of battle died.

My turn! In one brief second's thought
  I span the arc of changing years;
My heart goes out through boundless space,
  With choking, throbbing hopes and fears.
I think of one who, months before,
  Hung sobbing on my burning breast,
Whose words still linger on my ear:
  "My own; my heart's beloved, my best!"

I think of how, through weary days,
  I've stood, as now, before the gate,

And watched the human form within,
    Machine-like, serve the crowds that wait:
I think how, at the whispered name,
    His hand went deftly to the spot
Where life and death, and love and hate
    In waiting lay—but mine was not.

All this! but as the lightning's flash
    Before my eyes a missive lay;
A stranger hand—the seal unknown—
    What can this fearsome letter say?
God, give me but a moment's strength!
    Keep still, my heart—the seals are torn,
One line alone, the rest is dark—
    "She died at one o'clock this morn!"

A MILLION, ALL IN GOLD!

THE gallant ship went down at sea,
    Went down in the shrieking wind—
Went down with a hundred souls on board,
    And left no trace behind.
She was dashing—dashing grandly on
    Where the storm-swept waters rolled;
Her freight was a hundred beating hearts,
    And a million—all in gold!

The night was dark as a soul condemned,
    And the scream of the gale, despair.
The shivering crowds that clung to the shrouds
    Were raising their voices in prayer.
She rolled, in the dreadful trough of the sea,
    And their grip was a desperate hold,

As the ship went down with a trembling moan,
   And a million—all in gold!

The darkness closed on their one wild dirge,
   And the lightning gave one glare
On the spot where a group of ghost-like eyes
   Were fixed in a deathly stare!
But the morrow's sun shall kiss the place
   Where lie in the waters cold,
A hundred corses, stark and stiff,
   And a million—all in gold.

A thousand weary miles away
   Is a man with silvery hair,
Who bends o'er the desk in his counting-room,
   With a pale and frightened air.
He grasps the sheet that brought the news
   In a strong, convulsive hold,
And groans, "O God, the ship is lost,
   With a million—all in gold!"

Where flash the jewels in the light,
    And the music's master-tone,
With its rich, voluptuous, softening phrase,
    Makes heart and soul its own,
A wóman sits, superbly fair,
    And hears the story told;
She heaves a sigh for the glorious ship,
    And the million—all in gold!

A mother gropes at her daily toil
    Till her fingers cramp with pain,
But she knows that her days of care will cease
    When her boy shall come again;
But now her task will never be done
    Till she lies in the churchyard mould;
Her heart went down with the gallant ship,
    And the million—all in gold!

The mariner's wife has kissed her babe
    And hushed it with a song—

A song of hope and the coming time
    She has taught her heart so long.
She never will sing that song again,
    For the sailor stout and bold
Went down in the sea, with the foundered ship,
    And the million—all in gold!

And twice ten thousand careless eyes
    Shall read of the missing sail,
And twice ten thousand careless ears
    Shall listen to the tale.
And all that careless, listening crowd,
    The young, the gay, the old,
Shall speak of the fate of the gallant ship,
    And the million—all in gold!

There are other eyes and other ears
    Than that careless, listening crowd—
Eyes that are weeping endless tears,
    And hearts that cry aloud!

Hearts that shall cry for evermore,
   While the bells of life are tolled,
For the glorious ship that went to sea,
   With a million—all in gold!

DEATH'S CARRIAGE STOPS THE WAY.

MY Lady Clara, rich in grace,
And rich in all the charm of face,

Has marked her course upon life's way
With bold, imperious, haughty sway.

She walks embodied Fashion's queen,
The bowing ranks of life between.

She scorns the earth, rebukes the sky
With spurning tread and glancing eye.

And thus my lady goes her way,
Still stern and cold with every day.

My lady, lapped in luscious ease,
With all appliances to please,

Drove through the crowd that stood amaze
Behind her team of dappled grays;

Not thankful for the summer air,
But angered at the vulgar stare.

She sat in state to beauty blind,
And stately footmen clung behind,

While prudent hands her horses guide;
All this to feed my lady's pride.

But something checks my lady's course;
Amid the crush of man and horse,

Her carriage stands for moments still,
Against her fierce commanding will.

"Go on!" she cried with kindling face;
Who dares to stop my lady's pace?

"Go on!" she cried, yet pranced each gray,
Without proceeding on its way.

"Go on!" once more she cries in wrath;
"What minion dares to stop my path?"

Then hears her placid coachman say,
"Death's carriage, lady, stops the way."

Why grows my lady sudden pale?
Why do her stern commandings fail?

Among the guests who pass her door,
Has she ne'er heard that name before?

Nay! yes, full well she knows the name
Of him who once in welcome came,

Passed in her loveless, wedded door,
And loosed the fetters that she wore.

But now the mention made her start,
And checked the life-blood in her heart.

Death's carriage stops my lady's way,
While smiled the gorgeous summer day!

Her carriage moves, the moments fly,
And man and horse rush swiftly by,

But still my lady's stately pace
Keeps time with all her stately grace,

Until before her portal stays
Her stately team of prancing grays,

And stately footmen, from their height,
Descend to see my lady light.

Why comes she not? With wondering stare,
In silence, gaze the lackeys where

The open door invites approach
To help my lady from her coach.

At length, one bolder than the rest,
Stooped low, for once, his stately crest,

And peering to the cushioned deeps,
He whispered soft, "My lady sleeps!"

She sleeps, ay, sleeps the sleep of death;
His touch has chilled her stately breath;

His, the one power that dared to stay
My lady's carriage on its way.

MY PIPE.

WHAT! sell my pipe, sir? By old Jove!
    Ha! ha! excuse my ill-seemed mirth.
Why, boy, to get that pipe I clove
    A trooper to his saddle-girth!
What's that? Why, more than you have done,
    My white-faced lad, or you will do,
If you but end as you've begun:
    Mind what I tell you, lad, 'tis true!

Put up your money; this old pipe
    May be, as you have said, a gem:
Whoever loosens death's last gripe
    Will find it here, a prize to them.
A beauty! yes indeed, a pearl!
    See how the rich brown color glows;

The blushes of a pretty girl,
   The heart's core of the deep red rose!

Pshaw! sell my pipe! the thing's absurd!
   My silver-lipped, my amber-tipped!
See here, my lad, perhaps you've heard
   About a pack of fellows whipped
At Gettysburg? Well, I was there,
   Where showers of ball ploughed up the ground
Beneath the footsteps of my mare,
   Who challenged death at every bound!

Up came an order from our chief
   To take a belching battery nigh:
Our captain's words were sharp and brief,
   "Forward! which of ye fears to die?"
Like one united mass we sprang
   O'er abattis: the works were won;
With one wild shout the hillside rang,
   And then we spiked each murderous gun!

Just then a cloud of horsemen rushed
> Upon our rear like some fierce gust
By very count they should have crushed
> Our little band into the dust.
Full five to one the squadron came;
> Thank God! we knew not how to fly,
For, I'll be sworn, each felt the same,
> As men who did not fear to die.

Wild was the crash; the shrieks, the yells,
> The screaming of the frightened steeds!
It seemed as though a score of hells
> Had loosed their fiends for bloody deeds!
Each man of all our little band
> Fought like a hundred men in one,
Slashing his foes on either hand,
> As though 'twere but a bit of fun.

At last, with half our comrades slain,
> We beat the foemen wildly back,

And fiercely over hill and plain
    We smote them on their flying track.
My arm was hardened steel that day
    From shoulder to my sword's red tip;
But still, no blood was in the fray
    Of mine, save from my bitten lip.

But I had seen my brother fall—
    Hewed down by one great, giant blow:
The sight had turned my blood to gall,
    And almost checked its living flow.
I bent my mare's long reaching stride
    On every flying wretch I scanned,
Sworn that no spot on earth should hide
    The murderer from my vengeful hand.

The night was closing in around,
    With just enough of light to see,
When suddenly I heard the sound
    Of clattering hoofs not far from me.

I turned my mare, and stood on guard,
    My ready sabre on my knee;
My listening heart beat quick and hard,
    For something whispered, "This is he!"

I knew him at our horses' length,
    Though but a glimpse I had before—
His fierce, black eye, his size and strength,
    His hands all smeared with blackened gore;
And in his tightly clenchéd teeth
    He held this pipe with mocking grin—
A grin that hid a fiend beneath;
    A murderous fiend there lurked within.

He stretched his head, with straining eyes,
    Thinking my silent form a friend:
I marked him for a certain prize,
    And grasped my sabre for the end.
Just then he thrust his cursed face
    Far forward from his saddle-bow,

And with a puff lit all the place,
    And knew me for his deadly foe.

But ere his horse could backward spring,
    I clutched this pipe with fiercest hate;
Then, with one quick and desperate swing,
    My good sword fell—alas! too late!
He charged, and, in his fearful haste,
    He only took my bridle-arm;
I cut him, cleanly, to his waist:—
    An arm the less, boy, that's no harm!

So that's the way my pipe was won.
    Now, do you think I'd sell my prize!
Why, all the gold beneath the sun
    Would not so fill my loving eyes.
I kiss its bowl for memory's sake—
    The memory of my brother Steve;
It's presence keeps the thought awake
    Of him I slew that summer eve.

THE DYING SOLDIER.

STEADY, boys, steady!
        Keep your arms ready!
God only knows whom we may meet here.
Don't let me be taken:
        I'd rather awaken
To-morrow in—no matter where—
Than lie in that foul prison-hole over there.

Step slowly!
        Speak lowly!
These rocks may have life.
Lay me down in this hollow;
We are out of the strife.
By heavens! these fellows may track me in blood,
For this hole in my breast is outpouring a flood.

No! No surgeon for me, he can give me no aid;
The surgeon I want is a pickaxe and spade.
What, Morris, a tear? why shame on you man!
I thought you a hero; but since you've began
To whimper and cry, like a girl in her teens,
By George! I don't know what the devil it means!

Well! well! I am rough; 'tis a very rough school,
This life of a trooper, but yet I'm no fool!
I know a brave man, and a friend from a foe,
And, boys, that you love me I certainly know.
But wasn't it grand,
When they came down the hill, over sloughing and sand?
But we stood—did we not?—like immovable rock
Unheeding their balls and repelling their shock.

Did you mind the loud cry,
    When, as turning to fly,
Our men sprang upon them, determined to die?
    Oh! wasn't it grand!

God help the poor wretches that fell in that fight;
No time was there given for prayer or for flight:
They fell by the score in the crash, hand to hand,
And they mingled their blood with the sloughing and sand.
    Huzza!
Great heavens! this bullet-hole gapes like a grave;
A curse on the aim of that villainous knave!
Is there never a one of you knows how to pray,
Or speak for a man as his life ebbs away?
    Pray!
      Pray!

Thy kingdom come, thy will—why don't you
proceed?
Can't you see I am dying? Great God, how I
bleed!
Ebbing away!
    Ebbing away!
        The light of the day
        Is turning to gray.
           Pray! pray!
And forgive us our trespasses — tell me the
rest
While I stanch the hot blood from this hole in
my breast.
Say something to smooth the rough road I am
bound;
I am galloping fast over dangerous ground.
Do you think the good Master above will—-Pray!
pray!
Can't you see how my life-blood is ebbing
away?

Here, Morris, old fellow, get hold of my hand;
And, Wilson, my comrade — Oh! wasn't it grand
When they came down the hill, like a thunder-charged cloud,
And were scattered like mist by our brave little crowd?
Where's Wilson? My comrade, here, stoop down your head,
Can't you say a short prayer for the dying—or dead?

   Christ, God, who died for sinners all,
     Hear thou this suppliant wanderer's cry,
   Let not e'en this poor sparrow fall,
     Unheeded by thy gracious eye.
   Throw wide the gates to let him in,
     And take him pleading, to thine arms,
   Forgive, O Lord, his lifelong sin,
     And quiet all his fierce alarms.

God bless you, my comrade, for singing that hymn;
It is light to my path when my sight has grown dim.
I am dying—bend down, till I touch you once more—
Don't forget me, old fellow—God prosper this war!
Confusion to foes, but—keep hold of my hand—
But pray that peace comes to a prosperous land!

THE SAILING OF THE YACHTS.

UP pennon—heave the deep-sea lead;
    Our course lies to the sun:
God's grace to each stout mariner,
    Until the strife be done.
Between us and the restless waves
    An inch of plank stands guard;
White-bearded, and with threatening moans,
    They follow swift and hard.

With three proud colors in the air—
    The red, the white, the blue—
Three tiny vessels, trusting God,
    Away to eastward flew.
Stout hearts looked forward on the path,
    Nor dreamed mischance could be,

Such faith had each bold seaman in
   These graces of the sea.

Through blinding snow and cutting wind,
   In dreary winter-time,
They swept along the trackless deep
   Like some fierce Norseman's rhyme.
They sped as speeds the wild sea-bird
   When bursts the tempest wind;
They sped as speeds the swift narwhale,
   And leave the waves behind.

Sweeps down the icy northern blast
   Along their watery course,
Yet never dreams the seaman bold
   Of shipwreck or of loss.
His wishful eye is fondly bent
   Toward an alien shore,
And watchful for each offering gale
   To haste the journey o'er.

Speed on, ye tiny wingéd barks,
   By Yankee seamen manned,
And bear glad news through waves and wind
   To yon proud Eastern land.
Show them the blood from whence ye sprang
   Has in your keeping throve,
And that a native of your land
   Is one remove from Jove.

Show them that when your manhood wills,
   No winds can stop the way;
That angry waves but speed you on,
   By darkness or by day.
Show them that this same dauntless will
   That bore you to their shore,
Within the land you left behind
   Lives in a million more.

Show them that through our woeful pains
   Still throbbed the nation's heart;

That sword and bayonet has not
   Yet killed the nation's art.
Show them that through the deadly strife
   That rent us to the core,
We still had men enough to wield
   The hammer and the saw.

So be your mission one of joy
   To all the human race;
And hands that welcome you shall be
   The hands of courtly grace.
So shall your presence in the East
   Untie some Gordian knots,
And make the song of songs to be
   The "Sailing of the Yachts."

"RING DOWN THE DROP---I CAN-NOT PLAY."

OH! painted gauds and mimic scenes,
  And pompous trick that nothing means!
Oh! glaring light and shouting crowd,
And love-words in derision vowed!
Oh! crownéd king with starving eyes,
And dying swain who never dies!
Oh! hollow show and empty heart,
Great ministers of tragic art!

"There's that within which passeth show:"
The days they come, the days they go.
We live two lives, on either page—
The one upon the painted stage,

With all the world to hear and gaze,
And comment on each changing phase;
The other, that sad life within,
Where love may purify a sin.

Ring up the drop, the play is on;
Our hour of entrance comes anon.
Choke down the yearnings of the soul;
Weak, doting fool! art thou the whole?
The stage is waiting, take thy part;
Forget to-night thou hast a heart;
Let sunshine break the gathering cloud,
And smile thou on the waiting crowd.

Hear how their plaudits fill the scene:
Is not thy greedy ear full keen?
Is not a thousand shouts a balm
For all thy throbbing heart's alarm?
"To be or not to be"—the screed
Is listened to with breathless heed.

"RING DOWN THE DROP."

O painter with a painted mask!
Is thy brain wandering from thy task?

Can it be true that scores of years
Do not suffice to murder tears?
Can it be true that all of art
Has failed to teach the human heart?
Can gauds, and tricks, and shout, and glare,
The deafening drum, the trumpet's blare,
With all their wild, delirious din,
Not stifle this sad life within?

Pah, man! the eager people wait;
Go on with all thy studied prate.
Shall you not feed their longing eyes
Because—because a woman dies?
What cares the crowd for dying wives,
For broken hearts, or blasted lives!
They paid their money, and—they say—
Living or dead, on with the play.

"RING DOWN THE DROP."

What! staggering, man? why, where's your art?
That stare was good; that tragic start
Would make your fortune, were it not
That it rebukes the author's plot.
"My wife is dying!" He ne'er wrote
The words that struggle in thy throat.
"Take back your money," did you say?
"Ring down the drop—I cannot play."

Ring down the drop; the act is o'er;
Her bark has touched the golden shore,
While, reading from life's inner page,
Stands there the actor of the stage;
But not upon the cold, white corse
Falls there a word of sad remorse
From all that crowd who heard him say,
"Ring down the drop—I cannot play."

THE OLDEST PAUPER ON THE TOWN.

AND so old Betsey Green is dead!
   The oldest pauper on the town;
She who has eaten public bread—
   Bread of the most unchanging brown—
   For six-and-thirty years.

Old Betsey Green is under sod,
   Mixed in with loads of human clay;
No surpliced priest appealed to God,
   And challenged in the light of day
   A waiting crowd to tears.

They wrapped her lifeless, withered form
   In the scant sheet whereon she lay;
And while her limbs were lithe and warm
   They bore poor Betsey Green away,
   Lest she recover breath.

THE OLDEST PAUPER ON THE TOWN.

They nailed the county coffin down,
  With many jokes on her who died;
And one old pauper on the town,
  And only one old pauper, cried—
    From selfish fear of death.

A gravel-wagon bore the load,
  Unwashed, unswept from mud and mire;
The driver jolting o'er the road,
  Lest for the pittance of his hire
    He gave it too much ride.

And then the three-foot pauper-grave—
  Unwilling digged by pauper hands—
Where one—half idiot, half knave—
  With whitened hair, in waiting stands
    For Betsey Green who died.

He shovels in the frozen clods.
  He chuckles as they rattle down,
And to himself he laughs and nods—
  This oldest pauper on the town,
    Since Betsey Green is dead.

"I can remember well," he croaks,
 "That she was fair as any queen;
And well to do were all the folks
  Who were of kin with Betsey Green
   The day that she was wed;

"For all the maids in miles about
  Had set their caps at Robert Green—
The comeliest lad without a doubt,
  The country-side had ever seen—
   And she the greatest catch.

"And Betsey, she had babes as fair
  As though she'd chosen gifts for each:
They had their mother's eyes and hair,
  And Robert's wheedling treacherous speech:
   The selfish, greedy wretch!

"He spent the gold her father gave;
  He mortgaged all her broad farm-lands;
She toiled and watched, to earn and save:
  He never soiled his dainty hands,
   Or browned his handsome face.

"'Twas well for her, the neighbors said,
    When, on one cold, December day,
They found him, in a snow-wreathed bed,
    Upon the ice-bound public way,
        Fast locked in Death's embrace.

"For Robert loved the liquor-can
    . Too well to save his face or life:
The bloated semblance of a man
    Was all they brought the stricken wife
        From where he late had lain.

"Year after year, by day and night,
    Her hands and head were never still.
Her girls were fair, her boys were bright—
    Not one of all the six did ill,
        In wedding or in gain.

"Still, Betsey could not keep away
    The spectre who will never wait;
And so one stern and bitter day,
    She stood before the workhouse gate,
        To beg for pauper fare.

"Time flies! time flies! and Betsey's dead!
  And then, next comes my turn to die.
A hundred years were on her head—
  Ten years the elder she than I—
  How soon shall I be there!"

Again he stamped the frozen ground,
  With feeble step and vacant stare;
Cast one long, idle look around,
  And left old Betsey lying there,
  To wait her God and crown.

Ah, well! poor Betsey's pauper blood
  Runs proudly through some purple veins;
No base suspicion taints its flood,
  Of this, the worst of earthly stains—
  A pauper on the town!

DROWNED!

WHERE the mud lies black and slimy,
    Where the waters sweep along,
Where the wharfmen, stout and grimy,
    Heave and haul with many a song—
        Heaving still
        With a will,
Every coming dray to fill,
Hauling, with a laugh and shout,
Bales of wondrous size about;
Straining to the ponderous weight
Of the good ship's wealthy freight.

Where the wide and swelling river
    Rolls in one perpetual rhyme:

Where the gracious winds deliver
>Glorious things from every clime—
>>Stuffs to wear,
>>Spices rare,
Lie in heaps, or scent the air;
Where the merchant, full of gold,
Welcomes home the seamen bold;
Where each heart, its love confessed,
Clasps the loved one to the breast;

Where the soft-voiced land-breeze ever
>Hums its tune by mast and shroud,
Where the rough-tongued master never
>Ceases crying to the crowd—
>>"With a haul,
>>Lubbers all,
Stretch your muscles to the fall!"
Where the never-ceasing flow,
Man above, and waves below,

Night and day pours on and off,
Mingling at the city wharf;—

There the vagrant boy is standing
  With a ghastly, frightened air;
While each lounger is demanding
  What he sees to make him stare.
    Still his eyes
      Grow in size
As his stammering speech he tries;
And his finger points below,
Where the waters ebb and flow:
Still his lips give forth no sound
But a hoarsely-whispered "Drowned!"

Where the planks are green and rotten,
  Sending forth a sickening steam,
Where the daylight is forgotten,
  And the wharf-rat reigns supreme—

In his eyes

Fierce surprise

At his toothsome human prize:

Squeaking, gibbering forth a cry,

As the crash above goes by;

Heeding neither man nor horse

In his battles o'er the corse.

With a crowbar to the planking,

With the tackle and the fall,

With a heave, and with a clanking,

Shivering hands give willing haul.

There he lies!

Open eyes

Turned toward the sunlit skies;

There he lies in oozing slime,

Heedless of the place and time;

Heedless of the gazing throng,

Heedless of the clash and song.

Sunlight falls like shadows fading,
  Still the song goes on aloud—
Still with gaze that seems upbraiding
  Stares the dead man on the crowd.
    Hours fly
      Swiftly by;
Sunset darkens on the sky,
Ere the lingering men and boys
Hear the dead-cart's rumbling noise
O'er the distant stone-clad ground,
Coming for the man that's "Drowned."

Had his limbs been clothed in scarlet,
  Were his linen rich and rare,
Had he been the veriest varlet,
  Tainting God's own perfumed air,
    Would he lie,
      While hours fly,
Staring sightless to the sky?

Would the crowd so careless stand
If a gem gleamed on his hand?
Would they sing and laugh around,
Were he better dressed when "Drowned?"

THE SKATERS.

I STOOD on the frozen river,
    Watching the skaters go by;
They were laughing and shouting merrily
    Under the cold gray sky;
Lazily swinging their way along,
Cheerfully singing some snatches of song,
Skimming like birds on the face of the waves,
Swimming like fish in their deep-sea caves.

I saw not an eye but sparkled,
    Not a step but was careless and free;
They were laughing and shouting merrily,
    And as happy as happy could be;
Carefully staying the speed in their pace,
Warily weighing the chance in a race,

Winging their way through the change in the throng,
Singing the score of the SKATER'S SONG.

Over the ice, like the swallows, I fly,
With light in my heart and light in my eye;
The swiftest of runners their tardiness feel
When my feet are encased in the glistening steel.
  Away I dash,
    Like the lightning's flash,
Or the racer under the rider's lash.

Eyes that look out from the loveliest face
Laugh at my follies or smile at my grace;
The life of my blood courses up to the brain,
And the days of my boyhood come to me again.
  I look not back,
    Though the ice may crack,
For a hundred come like wolves on my track.

Up to the north, in the face of the gale,
Breathless we turn, spreading out for the sail;
A fleet of gay steamers rush down on the wind,
Leaving Time and the sluggards completely behind;
    For life but waits,
      At Pleasure's gold gates,
For the hours we spend on the glorious skates.

I stood on the frozen river,
    Watching the skaters go by;
They were laughing and shouting merrily,
    Under the cold gray sky;
Joyfully greeting the calls of a friend,
Heartily meeting the jibes they may send,
Kissing the lips of the loved ones that stay,
Missing the lips of the loved ones away.

There was one in the midst of the skaters,
    A beautiful boy of ten,

With a dreamy, dark-eyed beauty,
  Who flitted among the men;
Laughingly winning his way along,
Scarcely beginning to feel himself strong,
Stumbling and catching his step from a fall,
Tumbling and rolling about like a ball.

There was one in the crowd of watchers
  Who watched the boy in his play,
Whose eye was ever upon him
  Whenever he wandered away;
Smilingly gazing at each new start,
Silently praising the child in her heart,
Willing to follow the steps of her boy,
Filling her soul with his frolicsome joy.

I stood in the midst of the skaters,
  And looked at it all as a dream;
But my heart was suddenly wakened
  With a single death-like scream;

Fearfully filling the chill winter air,
Instantly stilling the song that was there,
Crushing the light from a thousand of eyes,
Hushing in terror a thousand of sighs.

    Where is the dark-eyed boy?
        And the ever-watching mother?
    A shrieking woman clings to her waist,
        And her hands are held by another;
Terribly standing, in accents wild,
Idly demanding her beautiful child,
Staring with eyes in a fire-like glow,
Tearing the lace from her bosom of snow.

    There is running to and fro,
        And the talking of many men;
    But an hour goes by before they find
        The beautiful boy of ten;
Quietly raising him under their breath,
Earnestly praising his beauty in death,

Putting his limbs in a natural way,
Shutting his eyes from the light of the day.

But the mother has broken her guard,
    And lies on the breast of her child;
  She is kissing the pallid, oozing lips
    That the waters have defiled;
Gloomily pressing the baby-like corse,
Fondly caressing, and mourning her loss,
Trying to waken the voice of the dead,
Crying to God for the soul that is fled.

  She has raised the babe in her arms,
    Rejecting all offer of aid;
  His arm falls over her shoulder,
    And his head on her bosom is laid;
Wearily bearing her burden of death,
Tenderly caring as though he had breath,
Creeping along with a staggering pace,
Weeping, and kissing the little pale face.

I stand on the frozen river,
    But the skaters no longer go by;
    They are gathered in groups at the landings,
    Under the cold gray sky;
Woefully talking of what they had seen,
Steadily walking where late they had been,
Running with terror at every sound,
Shunning the spot where the boy was drowned.

GIVE ME DRINK.

THERE'S my money; give me drink!
Fire to feed my hungry blood,
Drown my slightest wish to think:
    Give me drink!
Drench me in the burning flood,
Until life and soul are numb,
Until every pulse is dumb,
    Give me drink!
There's my clothing, there's my food,
Strip my limbs and leave them bare,
What care I how people stare?
    Give me drink!
They know not the fearful thirst
Of what they call the cup accursed—
The cup in which my brain's immersed;
    Give me drink!

GIVE ME DRINK.

There's my children, give me drink!
  Make me drunken in my heart;
I would sever every link,
  Ere my cup and I should part:
          Give me drink!
There is no nepenthe here,
Unhallowed by a woman's tear,
Unflavored with a wise man's sneer;
Their notice makes the draught more dear.
          Give me drink!
There's my health and peace of mind,
  I will give it all to thee,
I will throw my life behind,
  I will crouch upon my knee:
          Give me drink!
There's my wife—my wedded wife!—
Once I loved her as my life:
  What is wife and life to me?
          Give me drink!
Here's my standing as a man:

Give me drink!
Here's my Christian love and hope:
Give me drink!
Can I bear the social ban?
I can do what others can:
I can crawl, and steal, and kill,
So the draught be at my will—
Give me drink!
Here's my faith in all mankind:
Give me drink!
I scatter it upon the wind—
Give me drink!
And here—oh, here's my faith in God;
I will not bend and kiss the rod,
I'll trample Heaven iron-shod:
Give me drink!
Make me drunken in my brain,
  I will give thee wealth and fame;
Make me drunken in my heart,
  I will give thee spotless name:

GIVE ME DRINK.

    Give me drink!
Make me drunken night and day;
I will give my soul away,
God, and peace, and child, and wife,
Love, and faith, and hope, and life!
    Give me drink!

"IT WILL ALL BE RIGHT IN THE MORNING."

I STOOD by the couch of my darling,
    And watched the light in her eyes;
I held her fevered fingers,
    And echoed her softest sighs.
But the time wore wearily onward,
    Till it marked the sunset hour,
And the light went out from my darling's eyes,
    As the bloom goes out from the flower.

Ah! then with a sickening tremor,
    I watched for the soothing balm
That should come at the hands of the healer,
    And shield my love from harm.
It came at the hour of sunset:
    A grave and an aged man,

Who held the gift of a healing hand,
    As far as a mortal can.

He counted her pulses that fluttered
    Like wild imprisoned birds;
And then, with a glance to heaven,
    He spake these cheering words:
"It will all be right in the morning."
    Oh! skill of a learned leech,
Those words, to my worldly hearing,
    What a world of hope they reach!

"It will all be right in the morning!"
    I murmured them through the night,
As I watched her heavily breathing,
    And longed for the coming light.
It came with its golden sunshine,
    And I turned to my darling's bed,
To kiss her lips as a welcome,
    But I found my loved one dead.

Dead! Dead with the morning's coming,
    Dead! Dead with the words on my ear,
"It will all be right in the morning!"
    And now but her form is here.
O heart, in thy wild resistance
    At the stern decree of the Lord,
Rebelling to part with an atom
    From out of thine earthly hoard!

"It will all be right in the morning!"
    It was truth the wise leech spoke,
And in the heavenly sunshine
    My darling one awoke—
Awoke from a dream of sorrow,
    To dwell in the far-off lands,
Where, if all be right in the morning,
    Once more I shall clasp her hands.

GOD BLESS YOUR BEAUTIFUL HAND!

THE hand of my lady is soft and white;
    For the sculptor's skill a test;
The eyes of my lady are deep and bright,
    And her lips with kindness blest.

She moves with the grace of a crownéd queen,
    Who walks in a loving land,
But of all her charms the world has seen,
    There is none like her beautiful hand.

And I marveled much, for many a day,
    How the world so blind could be,
That it cast all her other charms away,
    And only the hand could see;

Until, as I sought a lonely street,
   One bitter December eve,
I heard the fall of my lady's feet,
   And a sad voice moan and grieve.

And then I saw her muffled form
   Draw nigh to a sightless elf,
And about it wrap, both close and warm,
   The shawl she had worn herself.

Then bending her head with a nameless grace
   To the beggar's outstretched palms,
She silently gazed in the hungered face,
   And gave it a queenly alms.

The old child caught at the fingers white,
   As though for a fierce demand,
And said, "Oh, what would I give for my sight!
   God bless your beautiful hand!"

Since then I marvel no more if the thought
  Should go through the length of the land,
And all that is proud of the earth shall have sought
  The charm of my lady's hand.

FARMER BROWN.

OLD Farmer Brown, with ruddy face,
    Sat stretched before the chimney-place;
He sat and watched the crackling logs,
The purring cat, the dreaming dogs,
That, like himself, were stretched at ease,
Safe sheltered from the chill night-breeze,
And with the freedom comfort brings,
The farmer thought these selfish things:

"Let foolish people grieve and sigh
    At care that does not come anigh;
I'm not so weak to wail at what,
However bad, concerns me not.
My barns are full with golden grain,
My limbs are stout and free from pain,

And out, as far as eye can see,
The well-kept fields belong to me.

"My appetite is always sound
Whene'er the dinner-hour comes round;
And faith, betwixt the wife and me
There's not much difference, as I see.
She's hearty, merry, stout and fair,
No touch of silver in her hair;
She grows, as years pass swift away,
Much better-looking every day.

"I read of cities lost and won,
Of deeds of bloody valor done,
Of fearful battles, fought in vain,
With scores of thousands for the slain;
Of ravaged homes, insulted wives,
And children fleeing for their lives.
But why should I repine at these
When they do not disturb mine ease?

"The blood shed in these fearful fights
Does not disturb my sleep of nights;
The thousands that they choose to slay
Take not my appetite away.
This mug of cider by my side
Does not across my palate glide
Less smoothly when the clash of war
Comes faint and harmless to my door.

"Then why should I repine, who ne'er
Am troubled with a single care?
Stop—let me think! Ah, yes, with one—
My wandering Will, my truant son—
He whom we loved, our darling child,
So handsome, kind, and yet so wild!
A word, regretted ere its birth,
Sent Will a wanderer o'er the earth.

"If Will were but at home again,
The world might war for me in vain.

A knock! Who's that? Come in? Ah, Jones!"
The farmer cried, in cheery tones.
'Walk in! Sit down! Here, wife, a light!
What brought you out this stormy night?
Why, man, your face is stretched as long
As any tramping beggar's song."

"Ah, Neighbor Brown, it grieves me sore
To enter thus your welcome door.
The news I bear is very sad:
Your son——" "Good Lord, what of the lad?"
"Your son was killed at Shiloh fight;
He died while battling for the right.
So, Neighbor Brown, bow to God's will;
He knows best when to save or kill."

Poor Farmer Brown, with starting eyes,
Stood now erect. With mournful cries,
"O Lord!" he said, "what have I done,
That thou shouldst take my only son?"

And then a something whispered loud,
"Thou selfish man, whom God endowed,
Take to thy heart this lifelong blow,
And learn to share thy fellow's woe!"

THE PATTER OF LITTLE FEET.

OVER my head, in the morning early,
    I heard the patter of little feet,
Rising above the hurly-burly
    Out in the fast-awakening street.
I like my nap in the morning early—
    That drowsy, sleeping, waking time—
And am apt to give way to a touch of the surly
    With one who breaks on its soothing rhyme,

And so this morn, when I heard the clatter,
    I turned uneasily in my bed,
And bothered my brain to guess the matter
    With the little ones pattering over my head.
My nap was gone, and in humor sulky
    I stretched a loud and imperious yawn,

And then, with a word both big and bulky,
  I blessed the hour those babes were born.

With a knitted brow and a hasty toilet,
  I made up my mind as I mounted the stairs,
Whatever the fun, I would quickly spoil it
  By coming upon them unawares.
I never had seen my top-floor neighbors;
  This only I knew, that the tidy house,
Save and except for these infantine labors,
  Was silent and still as a baby-mouse.

I knocked at the door, and a moment waited;
  The noise was hushed to a whispered word;
The patter of little feet abated,
  And a tiny hand on the knob I heard.
The door, with a labored opening, started,
  And full in its light a vision appeared,
That carried my heart to the days departed,
  And the one to whom it was ever endeared.

Oh, vision of life in the darkened palace
  Where I have enshrined the one of my love!
What vestige remained of the wrath and malice
  I threatened to wreak on the noise above?
What memoried thought is the one I am meeting?
  What hands are they stretched as I entered the door?
"Are you my papa?" was the baby-like greeting;
  "Are you my papa, come home from the war?"

"No, darling," I said, with a choking emotion,
  "I am not your papa, come home from the war;
I am only a waif on the fathomless ocean,
  With no one to love me the weary world o'er."
"With no one to love you?" the baby replies;
  "I will love you myself—you shall be my papa."

And I caught the sweet child with the wondering eyes
Up close to my breast where the memories are.

Oh, where was my heart as I lay in bed dozing,
And the noise overhead could not quicken its beat?
The chambers of memory surely were closing
When no entrance was found for those dear little feet;
For had I the riches we read of in story,
I would give up the whole to sweep away years—
To bring back the pleasure, the wealth and the glory,
The patter of dear little feet to my ears.

OLD NEWS.

OH! grandfather, grandfather, listen to me!
    The most wonderful news has come over the sea—
The most glorious news of the battles afar,
Where a million of men have been armed for the war.
From the field of Magenta the Austrians fled,
And a score of their thousands were left with the dead.
O'er the slopes of Palestro the conquerors bore
The eagles of France through a torrent of gore;
And the Austrian legions were swept in the gale,
As the husk is struck off by a blow of the flail.

Oh! grandfather, grandfather, read the great news;
It will tell you the chances for glory you lose;
It will tell of the joy for the victories won,
And the shouts of the nations for deeds that were done.
Dear grandfather, why don't you hurry away,
With your bright-bladed sword, to the midst of the fray?—
That bright-bladed sword which you said, in my hand,
Should some day strike blows for my own native land?
Oh! grandfather, what a great thing it would be
Could we both but have been in those fights over sea!

There were flashes of light in the grandfather's eyes,
And a chuckle that mingled itself with his sighs,

As he shook his white head, with a half-smothered groan,
And knocked out his pipe on the brown lintel-stone.
Ah! boy, it is one thing to strike for our lives,
For the land that we live in, our children and wives,
And another to battle with halters in sight,
Unknowing the quarrels that drive us to fight.
To cut and to slash at a despot's command
Is not fighting, my boy, for your own native land.

The echo that comes from the boom of the gun
Is lost in the shouts when the battle is done;
But the groans of the wounded and shrieks of the slain
Will be heard in the echoes again and again;

They will sound in the hearts, and be answered with tears,
When the field where they fell is grown over with years.
The news of a fight is like fresh-opened wine—
You must quench all your thirst while its bubbles still shine;
You must drink while the perfume is fresh on the breath,
For the dregs are a mixture of sorrow and death.

I fought, my brave boy, when to skulk were a shame
That could never be wiped from the line of a name;
I fought when refusal so blackened the youth
That his grandchild still blushes when told of the truth;

When the white hair of age marched proudly
    between
The iron-limbed man and the boy of fourteen;
When the crack of our rifles on Lexington plain
Was echoed, and echoed, and echoed again:
There were echoes, my boy, from the hills to
    the sea,
In the hearts of a million who longed to be
    free.

With us there was nothing of glitter and gold—
There was squalor and rags, and starvation and
    cold;
There were barefooted men, who were tracked
    by their blood
On the stone-jagged road or the icy-bridged flood;
There were men who had sworn by their foe-
    ravaged lands,
By their blood-darkened hearths, with their swords
    in their hands—

Who had sworn that their kindred should see
    them no more
Till the land should be free from the curse that
    it bore.
Those were times when the battle-field, gory and
    red,
Bloomed with flowers perpetual over the dead.

The news of those battles will never grow old—
They grow by the telling, a thousand times told;
But of fights that are fought for glory alone,
Ere the fighting is over the glory is flown.
It is dimmed on the crests of the conquering hosts
By the pale, bloody hands of a legion of ghosts;
It is washed from the blades of victorious chiefs
By the heart-sweating tears of a million of
    griefs.
Yes! even, my boy, from the head of a king
It is trampled and crushed like a valueless
    thing.

When the battle is over, the scarlet and gold
Shall speedily rot in the blood-nurtured mould;
The steed and his rider shall stay where they fall,
And the stout idle worm shall be master of all;
The rains shall wash down all the proud clotted gore,
And the winds bear away the last shreds of the war.
Yet, unless they have stricken for freedom and right,
The wails of the dying shall fade on the night;
But if God shall be with them, their hearts shall be bold,
And the news of their battle shall never grow old.

MISSING: PRIVATE WILLIAM SMITH.

SERGEANT! enter on your roll,
"Missing—Private William Smith."
Death is but a passing dream,
Life a false and shadowy myth.
Comrades, close your gaping ranks!
He was of the first platoon;
Missing Private William Smith
Doubtless will be heard of soon.

Missing Private William Smith
Led the charge that turned the day;
Through the thickest of the fight,
Step by step, he clove his way.
When I last saw Private Smith
He was grimed with smoke and gore,

What if Private William Smith
    Should be heard of never more?

Comrades! soldiers should not mourn.
    He was every inch a man!
Men have fallen in the fight
    Ever since the world began.
Yet I would I knew for truth,
    Now the fight is past and done—
Missing Private William Smith
    Has a wife and little one.

Would I knew that clanking chains
    Bound his iron muscles o'er!
Would I knew a prison wall
    Held his limbs, though wounded sore!
Would that missing Private Smith
    May be heard of once again!
Wounded, captive, so that he
    Be not of the nameless slain.

Missing Private William Smith
  Has a wife and little one;
She was once a love of mine,
  Ere my life had scarce begun.
I should hardly like to speak
  To her of so strange a myth,
When the war is over, as
  Missing Private William Smith.

I WISH THAT I COULD RUN AWAY.

DO you remember, chum of mine,
    How forty years, or more, ago,
In days when we were wont to whine
    O'er some tyrannic schoolmarm's blow?—
Do you remember one marked day,
    When, smarting from the birchen pain,
We packed our traps to run away;
    And run we did, with might and main?

Our wealth, in one newspaper rolled—
    Two shirts, two handkerchiefs, a top,
Two pairs of socks, grown somewhat old,
    And sundry ears of corn, to pop;
Two dozen marbles, several strings,
    Slate-pencils, and a choice whip-lash,

I WISH THAT I COULD RUN AWAY.

Three buttons, and some minor things,
    And nineteen cents in solid cash!

We wandered, that November day,
    At least four miles away from home,
When, just as we began to say,
    "How sweet it is to freely roam,
With every hedge a sheltering inn!"—
    There came a cold and drenching rain
That wet us to the very skin;—
    That night we slept at home again.

As time passed on, I thought and laughed
    At that sad escapade of ours,
And yet the thought would always waft
    A perfume, as of memoried flowers.
I find that with my growing years,
    With hair well-streaked with certain gray,
And all that time and taste endears,
    A strong desire to run away—

To run away and be at peace,
  With none to question, none to claim;
To shut away the world's caprice,
  Its turmoil, falsehood, and its shame;
To run away from struggling men,
  Who crush their brothers in the dust-
From ledger, cash-book, ink and pen,
  From cant, hypocrisy and lust.

To run from crowded cities, where
  The voice of man is never still;
To run from where the worm of care
  Is throned above Almighty will;
To run away to fields and flowers,
  And listen to the insect hum—
To lie forgetful of the hours,
  Forgetful of the time to come.

I sometimes think, good chum of mine,
  That day ill-chosen for our jaunt:

Should I again to run incline,
   'Twould not be in November gaunt,
But in the lusty summer-time,
   When birds and bees sing all the day,
When Nature seems a pleasant rhyme:
   That is the time to run away.

Believe me, that no sex or age
   Forgets that legend of its youth;
But, like a bird in gilded cage,
   Each pines for liberty and truth;
We writhe beneath some worldly pain,
   Refuse its mandates to obey;
Sigh for our childhood's days again,
   And wish that we could run away.

THE KISS IN THE STREET.

THE world is a world of glorious themes,
    The world is a world of wonder—
A web and a tissue of beautiful dreams,
    To be torn by the world asunder.
The world is an image of beauty,
    The world is a type of bliss;
If the world would but do its duty,
    There would be no world like this.

I walked on the street on a sunshiny day,
    I walked, and I watched the crowd—
The crowd that were looking so happy and gay
    That they almost shouted aloud.
I held by my hand my darling girl,
    She skipped and she danced along,

And, childlike, laughed at the hum and the whirl
    Of the countless moving throng.

I walked, and I watched the myriad mass
    That was sweeping idly by,
And it made me glad to see them pass
    With a smiling lip and a laughing eye.
And so I sang to myself a song—
    A song on the happiest theme—
To the crowd that was slowly passing along
    Like the mythical forms in a dream.

And so I sang as I walked along,
    Led by my baby guide,
And a man came out of the midst of the throng
    Who walked by my darling's side.
He was pale, and haggard, and marked with woe,
    But his clothes they were rich and fine,
And a diamond gleamed on his shirt of snow
    Which I wished at the moment were mine.

He walked for a while with a downcast eye,
  Then stooped with a sudden bow,
And I heard the moan of an inward sigh
  As he kissed my darling's brow.
In the crowded street we quietly stand,
  While neither offered to stir,
And he softly said, as he pressed my hand,
  "I have lost a child like her."

Then silently passed that haggard man
  To the midst of the crowd again,
And the song I had in my heart began
  Was hushed in a throb of pain.
It is many a year since that sunny day
  And my darling lives above;
The song and all have passed away
  But the memory of my love.

"I WOULD THAT SHE WERE DEAD!"

'TIS a night in the cold November,
   And I sit by a hearth of my own;
The fire is blazing brightly,
   But I sit by its blaze alone.
It is ten long years, I remember,
   This very self-same night,
I stood by this hearth-stone thinking,
   And gazed in the bright firelight.

That night of all nights I remember;
   I had drawn to my loving side
A girlish form in her beauty,
   And proudly I called her my bride;
And I loved her fondly and dearly—
   So dearly it seemed like a dream,

And I stood by this firelight thinking,
   While I pictured it out in the gleam.

There, far in the deepened shadow,
   I had built me a home of love;
In the midst of the lakes and the forests,
   With the sunny sky above,
I had children playing beside me,
   I had wealth and a true-hearted friend,
No care to press heavily on me,
   And all that the world could send.

And here, in the embers glowing,
   I wove me a wonderful name—
The name of a poet and patriot,
   With a world-wide whisper of fame.
But above all these pictures of glory
   There was one I had lain to my life:
This home was the case for the jewel,
   My darling and beautiful wife!

The years have run swiftly to nothing,
    And I sit by the fire and stare
In the glow of its embers vainly
    For what I once pictured there.
There is only a clouded changing,
    Where glimmers of light come out,
But before I can trace the picture
    They vanish and leave me in doubt.

Ah! where are those beautiful pictures—
    Those pictures I painted in light?
And why do I sit here lonely
    On this chilly November night?
'Tis a tale of terrible import;
    I tremble, and shudder, and start,
Whenever, by day or by darkness,
    I tell it into my own heart.

I worshiped her wondrous beauty,
    I praised it in sunshine and storm;

Her dream-like face in its glory,
  Her delicate roundness of form,
It was part of my love to tell it;
  I gloated on what I had won.
Oh, would that my tongue had been speechless
  Before the wild telling were done!

As soon would I thought to have doubted
  The Source of eternal life
As the purity, truth and honor
  Of my young and my beautiful wife.
O God! in thy mercy save me
  From the memory of that day
When she fell from her truth and honor,
  And passed from my side away.

I have stood by the bedside cursing,
  With my soul in a tumult wild,
When you took, in your gracious wisdom,
  My only, my heart-born child.

As much, O God! as I loved her,
    I bend to your stern decree,
Though it tears out my soul when I say it;
    She is better in heaven with thee.

I have sat by this fireside trembling,
    While the wealth I had madly won
Was passing away from my keeping,
    Like mist from the morning sun.
It was something to mourn for a moment,
    But I lived in the world alone,
And I gave up the gold and my trembling
    With a single silent moan.

I have drank from the cup of sorrow,
    And eaten the bread of shame,
But of all that has passed before me,
    I was still in my heart the same.
But oh! this day thou hast crushed me—
    This day, of all days of the year,

Thou hast left me here by my fireside,
  With a shivering, deadly fear.

This day I have seen the woman
  Who lay on my bosom for years—
The woman I worshiped in sunshine,
  The woman I worshiped in tears.
She was old, and wan, and haggard—
  I would that this saying were all;
But—she wore a dress that I gave her—
  I gave her—before her fall.

It was ragged, and torn, and drabbled,
  But I knew in an instant again
The horrible shade of each color
  That burned to my quivering brain.
I have seen her the star of the evening,
  Wearing that robe of death,
When my heart overflowed with the praises
  They spoke of her under the breath.

She was old, and wan, and haggard;
  She was bleared, and drabbled, and torn;
But she was not worse than I am,
  With the light of my life all gone.
I shut my eyes on the vision,
  And I bowed my stricken head;
I only uttered one silent prayer—
  "I would that she were dead!"

I am sitting here in the firelight,
  But I cannot trace a line;
The woman I loved in years agone
  Stands with her life in mine.
God, in thy mercy, listen to me,
  Ere the light of my soul be fled—
Listen, and grant this single prayer—
  "I would that she were dead!"

WHAT I SAW.

AM I paler than is my wont, my love?
    Let me lay your head on my breast;
There is quiet truth in your dark brown eyes—
    In the eyes that I love best.
You can twine your arms about my neck,
    And believe me all your own,
While I tell the cause of my whitened cheek
    To you, my love, alone.

There is sunshine on the crowded street
    And the day is superbly fair;
There are beautiful women in jewels and gold
    Wandering grandly there.
There are blooded teams that spurn the stones,
    Tossing their heads to the wind;

Carriages covered with pomp and glare,
    Cushioned and satin-lined.

There was one I marked for the silken shine
    Of its proudly-stepping bays,
Till she who sat in its cushioned depths
    Broke full on my startled gaze.
It was Madaline—she whom I loved so well—
    Draw thyself nearer to me—
When I was a boy, and she was a belle,
    And I was a stranger to thee.

She would let me hold her smooth white hand
    Till I shivered with passionate dread;
She would press her burning lips to mine
    While I held her beautiful head.
Yes! while I held her head to my breast,
    Just where your own now lies—
Twine your arms closer about my neck,
    And look me full in the eyes—

She said that she loved me better than life,
   But ah! not better than gold;
You have heard the story a thousand times,
   It is very, very old.
He cannot wipe from her crimson lips
   One single passionate kiss;
He cannot blot one burning word:
   Does he ever think of this?

Does she ever think of the wonderful love
   That held her above the skies?
Does her frozen heart give no response
   From its tissue of living lies?
Yes! I watched her eyes as they met my own,
   Her cheek was far paler than mine;
I had bountiful time, as she dashed along,
   To compare her beauty with thine.

She will never forget that autumn day
   When she kissed my cold, clinched hand;

When my trembling passion was crumbled away,
  In a moment, at her command.
I had terrible thoughts that autumn day,
  As I stood by the waves of the sea,
But oh how deeply I thank her now
  For the words she spoke to me!

Lay your head close to my beating breast:
  Madaline married for gold.
Do you feel my heart how warm it is?
  Madaline's heart is cold.
The look I gave her that autumn day
  Has frozen its every vein;
Madaline never will know what it is
  To love or be loved again.

Now you may know, my own sweet love,
  The reason my cheek grew pale;
I have looked on the terrible gulf I have passed,
  When borne on the blast of the gale.

Madaline—she has jewels and gold,
　And silks of a gorgeous hue;
I have, myself, a beating heart,
　And you, my love, and you.

"PLEASE HELP THE BLIND."

WITH vacant thought and wandering step,
   One warm September day,
I walked, where thoughtless thousands walk,
   Along the bright Broadway.
And on the thoughtless thousand ears,
   Borne by the autumn wind,
There came, above the crash and roar,
   A moan—"Please help the blind."

Where all the countless crowd went on,
   By silken garments swept,
There sat a man whose changeless face
   Would seem as though he slept.
His stolid form was clad in rags,
   His eyes to heaven inclined,

And from his scarcely moving lips
    He moaned, "Please help the blind."

O God! how struck the dismal cry
    Upon my wearied heart!
How quick compelled, in every vein,
    The sluggish blood to start!
An echo sprang within my soul,
    With all my years entwined,
And mingled with the hopeless moan:
    O Lord! "Please help the blind."

"Please help the blind" whose failing years
    Point past the dream of life;
Whose hearts and eyes are closed alike
    To misery and strife.
Who, blinder than the beggar blind
    That pleads upon Broadway,
Have shut alike their eyes and hearts
    And thrown their lives away.

"Please help the blind" whose pride of place
    Hath kept their thoughts above
The treasure of an earthly rest,
    The purity of love.
Who, by their wandering in the world,
    Have lost the light of home,
And now, with cold, contracted steps,
    In utter blindness roam.

"Please help the blind" who, through the years
    You gave them for their kind,
Have stretched abroad their greedy hands
    As grope the veriest blind.
Who know no end but lands and gold,
    And now, when comes the night,
Moan prayer on prayer through weary hours
    For but a moment's sight.

And while my prayer ascends on high,
    Hear thou the saddened cry

Of one who walks in blindness on,
   While all the world goes by;
Who hears the moan upon Broadway,
   Yet fails the path to find,
And echoes in his heart of hearts,
   O Lord! "Please help the blind."

SOMEWHERE TO GO.

'TWAS on a moonlight Sunday eve,
    In warm October time,
I sat alone, and listened to
    The calling churchbells' chime,
And every one that reached my ear
    Were stranger bells to me,
For I was in the stranger's land,
    Far o'er the distant sea.

I took my glass from off the wall,
    I gazed into its deeps,
And pondered, as I thought of Time,
    How stealthily he creeps.
The wrinkles mark my sunken cheek,
    The silver tinge my hair,

My eye has lost its lustre now,
   And speaks a world of care.

Ah, me! I cannot help the thoughts
   The chiming bells will bring—
Those Sabbath eves when I was young
   And happy as a king.
The sorrow now that swells my heart
   I had not learned to know,
And every Sunday night that came
   I'd somewhere then to go.

I have a memory to-night
   That fills my lonely room—
A sunny face, a winsome smile
   That lightens up the gloom;
I have a memory of an eye
   That made my own to glow,
On Sunday nights, in times when I
   Had somewhere I could go.

SOMEWHERE TO GO.

On Sunday nights, with extra care,
    I stood before my glass,
And studied that I should not let
    An imperfection pass.
I dressed for eyes that thought me quite
    A model of a beau,
And merry were the Sunday nights
    I'd somewhere I could go.

I have a memory of some curls
    That often swept my cheek,
A head that pressed my bosom till
    I lost the power to speak.
I have a memory of an arm
    As white as driven snow,
That clasped my neck on Sunday nights
    When somewhere I could go.

For I was young, and she was pure,
    And all our dream was love—

I thought my gentle Abigail
  An angel from above.
The future was a casket locked,
  It opened sure and slow,
And closed upon the Sunday nights
  When somewhere I could go.

Ah! well, the time has passed away,
  And I am here alone;
And baby Abbie, whom I loved,
  Has seven of her own.
The dark-brown curls that swept my cheek
  Have lost their 'wildering flow;
'Tis thirty years of Sunday nights
  Since I could somewhere go.

Yet 'tis a pleasant memory,
  Though I am here alone,
To know my gentle baby-love
  Has seven of her own.

For I am sure amid those loves
　My own must slightly glow,
As she recalls the Sunday nights
　When I—could somewhere go.

Then let the years roll swiftly by,
　And leave me here alone,
To listen to the chiming bells
　Of unfamiliar tone.
I'll live upon the memories
　That in my bosom grow,
Though Sunday nights may come, and I
　Have nowhere now to go.

SWINGING IN THE DANCE.

WE met where harps and violins
    Were singing songs of mirth;
Where creatures floated in the space
    Almost too fair for earth.
We moved amid the surging crowd,
    And by one single glance
My heart was lost, for ever lost,
    While swinging in the dance.

We met where woods and waters meet,
    Where birds the music made,
And to her listening eyes and ears,
    My love-lorn tale I said.
I asked my pardon from her lips,
    For this, love's first advance,

And that she would return my heart,
Lost swinging in the dance.

We met beneath the sacred dome
To consecrate our love,
And these words came, as though they had
Been whispered from above:
"My darling, I could not return
Your heart, lost by love's chance,
But I can give you mine instead,
Won swinging in the dance."

NOTICE.

This volume being a new and enlarged edition, the publishers feel it incumbent on them to say something in reference to certain of the poems therein contained, especially the leading poem of "Beautiful Snow."

This fine poem has had the singular literary fate of having been claimed by no less than eight or nine different persons, several of whom have actually disputed with the real author through the public press and with the publishers, ending only in their shame and the conviction of falsehood.

"Beautiful Snow" was written by Mr. J. W. Watson—who has for twelve years been known in the first literary circles of New York, and who has held leading positions on the daily and weekly press of that city—while on a visit to Hartford, in November, 1858, and published in "Harpers' Weekly" immediately afterward. The poem having achieved a wonderful popularity in this country and in Europe, and in its traveling through the press become mutilated, we, knowing the real author, purchased through him, of Messrs. Harper Brothers, the copyright, and published it in this enduring form. Its great sale has warranted our belief in its popularity and its fast increasing appreciation.

That all false claims and falsehoods might be set at rest, we have combined with it several more of Mr. Watson's poems, which will show by their beauty, and the style, that they are all from the same hand.

"The Sailing of the Yachts" was written at the time of the famous ocean yacht race, and was thought by the "New York Herald" worthy of insertion in its editorial pages.

"Ring Down the Drop, I Cannot Play!" was written after a circumstance that occurred several years since at the Terre Haute theatre, where Mr. McKean Buchanan and his daughter were playing, and simply follows his words and tells the story as it occurred.

"The Dying Soldier" is another poem that has achieved wonderful popularity; and it is a fact worth mentioning that this poem and "Beautiful Snow" were read upon one night, a few months since, to audiences ranging from one thousand to four thousand, in seven of the great cities of the country, including New York, Philadelphia and Boston.

The universal press of the country received the first edition of this volume with the highest commendation, and especially spoke of "The Patter of Little Feet," "The Oldest Pauper on the Town," and "Farmer Brown," and of Mr. Watson as a poet of the highest order, and one who appeals directly to the human heart.

In issuing the present edition, several other poems written by Mr. Watson have been added to it, viz.: "The Kiss in the Street," "I would that She were Dead," "What I Saw," "Please Help the Blind," "Somewhere to Go," and "Swinging in the Dance." These poems possess great interest, and display a lively and pleasant fancy, as well as a genuine, hearty sympathy with the joys and sorrows of humanity. They will take strong hold of the heart and memory, and will live and last because they touch many chords of human sympathy.

www.ingramcontent.com/pod-product-compliance
Lightning Source LLC
Chambersburg PA
CBHW020111170426
43199CB00009B/484